Six-Word Lessons for a
GROWTH MINDSET

100 Lessons for Personal Growth Using *Forward Principles*

Rae Ann Hall

Published by Pacelli Publishing
Bellevue, Washington

Six-Word Lessons for a Growth Mindset

All rights reserved. No part of this book may be reproduced or transmitted in any form or by any means, electronic or mechanical including photocopying, recording or by any information storage or retrieval system, without the written permission of the publisher, except where permitted by law.

Limit of Liability: While the author and the publisher have used their best efforts in preparing this book, they make no representation or warranties with respect to accuracy or completeness of the content of this book. The advice and strategies contained herein may not be suitable for your situation. Consult with a professional when appropriate.

Copyright © 2019 by Rae Ann Hall

Published by Pacelli Publishing
9905 Lake Washington Blvd. NE, #D-103
Bellevue, Washington 98004
PacelliPublishing.com

Cover and interior designed by Pacelli Publishing
Cover image by Pixabay.com
Author photo by Jennifer Boyle Photography

ISBN-10: 1-933750-98-7
ISBN-13: 978-1-933750-98-9

Dedication

To my mom, who is a true warrior!

Acknowledgements

I want to thank the many people in my life who have taught me universal principles, exemplified living their purpose with passion, and encouraged me to do the same.

- ❖ My brother Mike for being an example of strength in resilience

- ❖ My husband Russ for his strong ethics, character and unending support

- ❖ My greatest mentor, Doyle Stokes, who is an example of living in strength, serving and caring about others consistently

- ❖ My angel girl Amelia, who exudes courage, strength and compassion daily

To the strong women in my life who push me to be better, both by their example and by their encouragement: Suzanne Hall, Diana Hill, Dani Green, Wendy Leyva, Amity Addrisi, Kerstin O'Shields, Brenda Reiss, Diana Ruiz and Jill Roundy.

Contents

Introduction 7
Accept Where You Are Right Now 11
Intentionally Go through Each Day Consistently 23
Your Center of Strength and Light 35
Be Accountable for Your Own Actions 47
Be a Champion of Resilience Mentality 59
Embrace Your Differences and Unique Self 71
Seek Help and Implement Advice Wisely 83
Set and Achieve Goals on Purpose 95
Be Comfortable with Success. Own it! 107
Give Back to Community and Others 119
   Note from the Author 130
   About the Six-Word Lessons Series 131

Introduction

"Real focus on your thoughts will lead to greater results in your aspirations and help you access the incredible strength that already resides within you."
--Rae Ann Hall

You are powerful beyond measure, and you have so much inner strength. I encourage you to tap into it daily, and the tools in this book will help you do that. Your mindset and belief about your own worth, core values, life's possibilities, and purpose will drive the results in your life. The inspiration for this book is to share *Forward Principles* that will help you continually build a growth mindset and access your inner strength, managing emotions that could detour you.

When life throws you curve balls, it will no longer rock your world.

You will experience greater joy and fulfillment when applying these true principles in your life.

You will have a strong sense of self and strength to shine brightly and be in alignment with your priorities.

What are *Forward Principles*?

FORWARD PRINCIPLES are practical steps to build a solid foundation in which you can build a fulfilled life through tapping into your inner strength and creating a growth mindset. They are actionable ways to intentionally move forward in a positive way. Each chapter in this book is related to a *Forward Principle*.

First: BE IN THE PRESENT - This is about getting into the present with where you are now. Accepting yourself in the here and now. The person you are today is the person you have to work with to get where you are going. Honor yourself, believe in yourself and get going after it.

Second: INTENTIONALLY FACE EACH DAY - As your values and priorities align, approach each day with intention and strength. Embrace your vision, values and mission statement. Fill yourself up with motivation and planning with focus.

Third: YOUR SOURCE OF LIGHT AND STRENGTH - Explore and find your greatest source of strength and light to consistently fill yourself up with good energy. This will continue your growth daily and feed your mind, body and spirit.

Fourth: BE ACCOUNTABLE - Accepting full accountability for your own thoughts, feelings and actions will amplify your ability to access your inner strength as well as live with purpose. This will change your mindset and the trap that can come by staying focused on the things you cannot control and moving on to the things you can control--your thoughts and actions.

Fifth: RESILIENCE MENTALITY - Resiliency is imperative in moving forward, you will have ups and downs, we all do, it's a part of life. Facing the setbacks with intention is key for gaining continued inner strength and maintaining positive self-image. Seek help and implement the advice you are getting, using your wisdom while still being challenged to embrace new ideas that will break limiting beliefs.

Sixth: EMBRACE YOUR UNIQUE SELF - Embrace who you are, good and bad, be authentic and claim your unique brilliance.

Seventh: WISELY CHOOSE SUPPORT - Seeking out a mentor and coaching will help you keep going and progressing. Surround yourself with uplifting people who live enlightened and are forward-minded.

Eighth: GOALS AND ACTION PLAN - Inner strength comes from continued progress, including setting and achieving goals, reaching higher levels and building up to bigger goals as you put your strengths to work and build on your successes each step of the way. Accomplish and expand your greater self by having a clear vision and seeing in your mind's eye the desired outcome--what it will take.

Ninth: EMBRACE THE FEELING OF SUCCESS - As you start to see success and access your inner strength, embrace your accomplishment and keep it going! It is so important to claim the progressive life that results from intentionally moving forward and achieving goals, embracing the light and your successes. You want to move forward gaining more and more confidence in your purpose so you can live inspired and with passion.

Tenth: SERVICE AND GIVING BACK - Giving back deepens the whole experience of life. Serving others promotes healthy feelings of contributions that are win-win. It can clear out a cluttered mind and dispel the negative effects of being self-involved. It is also sharing your strength which leaves you with a meaningful feeling inside, and a sense of fulfillment.

Accept Where You Are Right Now

1

Pay attention to your focused thoughts.

Being present with where you focus your thoughts is the best place to start, because that is the greatest influencer in your life. What are you focusing your thoughts on consistently? Once you get clear on that, you will have a place of reference for what created the feeling and influenced your decisions, which then propelled your actions and gave you the outcome from your efforts.

Think and see the situation differently.

Take a breath and step away from the emotion of the situation so you can see it more clearly. What thoughts were going through your mind at the time? Your thought influenced your emotion which fueled your action. If you calm your mind when you are starting to feel an overwhelming emotion, you can give your brain new thoughts to go to work for you, getting the result you desire.

Breathe out negative and limiting beliefs.

Breathing techniques will be beneficial in letting go of negative feelings and even limiting beliefs. Breathe in deeply, think of new life, hope and light, visualizing your best life. As you exhale, visualize the release of the tension and negative energy, letting go of limiting beliefs that bind you down. It works! Release, replace, repeat.

Know the past doesn't define you.

Claiming where you are right now and being present in no way means you are stuck there. Your setbacks and prior situations do not define you, how you move forward does. This is part of your journey and as you push forward, you will inspire others to do the same. You are liberated when you see your potential and live your purpose.

5

How you move forward cultivates hope.

As you do things to feed your mind, body and spirit, it will propel you toward a more fulfilled life, and you will begin feeling more and more hope. Embrace the hope that comes when you decide to not stay stuck in the past. Embrace light and be filled with hope for the life you are creating.

Build on hope to cultivate belief.

Being filled with hope will cultivate a more positive outlook. You will begin to build more belief in yourself and the good in the world. You will begin to believe that your dreams are possible, and that your life has meaning and purpose.

7

Turn belief into passion for present.

The momentum of hope and belief will begin to fill you with passion. Especially as you see your best life in sight and are pushing forward. The present day begins to be lived on purpose with intention and clarity. Fuel that passion into your daily activities and you will grow exponentially.

Develop a strong sense of self.

Put great effort into developing a strong sense of self, one intentional thought at a time, going after your hopes, dreams and aspirations daily. You are of great worth and add so much value to the world! You've got this, so go get after it! Do you see it and believe it? Then you can achieve it!

9

Forgiveness is key in moving forward.

Forgiveness is freeing and will release unwanted negative emotions that may be holding you back. It is a process and a journey. For you to feel at peace and be free of anger, bitterness or hate for something that may have happened to you, forgive so you can be set free. Forgiving the person isn't keeping them in your life. Forgive, move on and keep safe boundaries.

10

Envision possibility of a positive future.

What we think about, comes about. The mind can achieve what it sees. Take time to envision what is possible, what will be, what can be, and what good you will do. Envision the right people coming into place to put things in motion for you living your purpose and passion. Your vision and how you see yourself, even the future, is what ignites it coming to fruition.

Intentionally Go through Each Day Consistently

Begin your day with intentional strength.

How you start your day will set the tone for the day. Begin the day intentionally, tapping into what gives you the most strength and fills you up inside. This will give you more energy that you will be using to giving to others and projects. You can't give what isn't in you. Nurturing yourself and filling up with extra strength will help you stay on course and make it through.

Each day is a growth opportunity.

Good and bad things come up throughout the day. Have the attitude that they are learning experiences to keep growing. Set the tone for the day, make the best choices you can, be intentional on your tasks, but know that things are going to happen. These things will be different each day and facing them will prepare you for future opportunities, even dealing with situations that may come up again.

# Focus on your day with purpose.

Take time to plan your day with focus. Start with your purpose, being clear on who you are and what you can accomplish (mindset). Write out all the tasks you need to complete and number or code them in order of importance and priority. Keep it simple but intentional. You will accomplish more when you have belief in self, intention, purpose, and priorities. Include self-care through exercise and healthy eating.

Decide how to face setbacks now.

As the bumps in the day come, and they usually do, adjust and move forward. When you decide ahead of time how you will respond in those moments, you handle it much better. Some days are smooth, and others have surprises. Either way, decide now how you will respond, and what you will do to not let it distract or destroy your purpose and priorities.

15

Each day builds on your strength.

Just like a house is built one brick at a time, your life is built one thought, one decision, and one action at a time. Be intentional and productive with each thought and your interactions with others. Each day you apply these principles and keep moving forward, you will continue to get more strength which will turn into even more strength, building a strong life.

Be flexible without giving up purpose.

If you have important things and sometimes family emergencies that come up during the day, of course you will be flexible and move that up the priority list. Keep your focus and purpose, rearranging what you can to stay on task and keep your integrity. You will find the solution. Be careful not to let other people's lack of preparation become an emergency for you.

17

Reflect on what went right today.

A great way to continue building confidence, hope and inner strength is to reflect daily on your wins. Take time to acknowledge all the good that came into your life today and how you lived in alignment with your priorities, even handling setbacks. Celebrate the strength and progress you see in yourself. Journal your strength attributes on display today and the great things you accomplished.

18

Stretch, relax and journal your day.

A great way to unwind from the day is to do stretching exercises. They clear your body of tensions and your mind of stress. Journaling your wins, activities, insights and thoughts of the day is a great way to keep you moving forward, building on strengths. Ending your journal entry with something you are grateful for keeps the positive mental attitude and helps cultivate a positive outlook, building inner strength.

End days in love and appreciation.

Love gives you light and energy which brings healing and peace. Take a moment before your head hits the pillow to fill yourself with love and light from your source of strength, appreciating the gifts received that day. Whether it is praying, reading or meditating, you will be strengthened and find inner peace as you fill yourself with love. Self-love is a necessary component to inner peace and truly living as your greater self.

Six-Word Lessons for a Growth Mindset

20

Envision best self when closing eyes.

As you lie in bed, a great practice is to envision your best self and your best life. See yourself achieving your goals and feel what it is like to be that person in the moment of truly living your best life and fulfilling your passion. If you can see it, you can achieve it. Let it become a part of you and let your mind claim it.

Your Center of Strength and Light

Turn to your source of light.

What is your greatest source of light and strength? Take time to discover it. When you find what truly feeds your soul beyond your own power, tap into it often. Knowing what your center of strength is and embracing it, fills your soul up with hope, energy, strength and light.

Be firm in your belief system.

Find out what makes you feel centered and connected to your energy source. What are your core values, principles and beliefs? Discover or rediscover who you are and what makes you motivated. Stay true to your convictions and live by them. As you live what you believe, you will have integrity and attract good things to you. Inner peace, stability and strength come from living in alignment with your core beliefs.

Find inner strength through daily meditation.

Take time to meditate and be one with your thoughts, connecting to enlightenment from your source of light. This is crucial in nurturing your soul and filling up with good energy. It will give you strength, cultivating inner peace. Meditation will help you have trust again and invite love into your heart. Walking every day and pondering on things helps your body and mind.

24

Quiet the noise in your home.

Too much noise in your home creates chaos. Quieting the noise in your home will calm your mind and help you focus on productive thoughts. Also, the wrong kind of noise in your home can bring darkness. You want to create an atmosphere in your home that is calm, fun, and filled with light. Open the shades, de-clutter and keep it clean. It really helps you feel better.

25

Avoid taking on another person's chaos.

Compassion and helping others is worthy, that is not what we are addressing here. Chaos is random and uninvited. If someone starts dumping their worries and anger on you, you have a choice to stay in that moment, or kindly exit. Take a call, go to the bathroom, or straight-up tell them you are not in a place to help them with the situation.

Tap into strength through breathing techniques.

Breathing techniques are great because you can do them anywhere and at any time to bring down the stress level or just get recentered. Breathe in deeply, hold and then exhale; you will feel your body relax and your mind clear. You can even experience a reduction in heart rate and blood pressure when you take deep, slow breaths for ten minutes a day.

Remind yourself that you are worthy.

Your self-talk and belief in yourself is fundamental in developing and maintaining a growth mindset. When you take time regularly to appreciate and fully understand your great worth, you fuel your self-image, connecting to your infinite worth and getting past any negative thoughts or feelings.

Kindly exit situations that contradict beliefs.

With all the work on finding your belief system and living your core values, protect them and exit situations that are taking you away from your center. In keeping your convictions and controlling your surroundings the best you can, you will stay more connected to inner peace. You have a choice about what you invite into your mind and the environment you choose to be in will protect that.

Find a place to quietly recenter.

Find a few places at home, work, or school where you can be with your thoughts and have quiet time. Five minutes in silence alone can recharge you from the things happening around you or the people around you. Avoid becoming drained and feeling empty by the end of the day by taking time throughout your day to breathe and get centered with your source of light.

Be in the moment through grounding.

When overwhelming things are happening in the day, grounding can help you work through them, bringing you back to a centered place. A Robert Frost poem says, "the best way out is always through." Suppressing the feelings is not healthy. Find a quiet place where you can feel what you are feeling, and emotionally and logically make your way back into the present. Research grounding techniques that will work for you.

Be Accountable for Your Own Actions

Be known for keeping your commitments.

Integrity and inner strength begin with keeping your word. You cannot control the actions of other people, but you can control your thoughts and actions. It is important to be accountable for your own actions daily, to keep building your strength base and confidence. Stay away from blaming, own who you are and live with integrity. Keeping commitments builds integrity.

Speak and live truth, never lying.

Integrity is also speaking the truth. Inner strength and confidence in self is experienced when you are at one with your core values and living an honest life. Dishonesty tears down people, families and organizations. Believe in your worth; nothing needs to be embellished or exaggerated. You can face mistakes and own up to your part. In fact it propels you forward. Honesty cultivates trust and a guilt-free feeling.

Accept responsibility when you make mistakes.

Minimizing your part will keep the mistake happening. Often it is simply owning your mistake that helps you move forward and see it for what it is, a learning opportunity. Every person in this life makes mistakes. Look at the situation, see what you did wrong and own it. When you focus on what you did, you can do something about it.

Place the mask on yourself first.

Nurturing yourself with love and kindness fuels you to give your best and be there for your friends and loved ones. Developing talents, building on your strengths, self-care and positive mental attitude all take continued effort. It is necessary for filling yourself up and creating the type of person you want to be.

What am I doing wrong now?

Self-check to stay on course. When you make mistakes, assess what might be going wrong and what decisions you are making that are leading you down the wrong path. The first step toward change and progress is to acknowledge what might be going wrong so you can do something about it. This isn't a beat-yourself-up moment, it's a simple assessment to lovingly course-correct.

What am I doing correctly now?

When self-checking, observe all the good you are doing and the great decisions you are making. See your progress which will consistently add to your growth mindset. Build on your strengths, creating what you want. When you feel good about where you are and what is going right, your outlook is good, and you will do good in the world.

ns.

Look for your part in conflict.

Take ownership of your part in any conflict because that is all you can do something about. If the other person lacks integrity and doesn't own their part, that is on them and you cannot change that. Focusing on the other person is wasted energy and produces nothing for your growth mindset. You can also lose valued friends by only seeing what they did wrong.

Keep your behavior in check consistently.

You decide how you are going to behave. Being consistent with your behavior develops trust in yourself and people know you are trustworthy. Don't try for perfection, just consistent behavior in line with your morals and values. In stressful moments, use grounding and breathing techniques to calm and recenter yourself. Focus your thoughts on what produces good results, which will influence your feelings and actions.

You control your thoughts and mindset.

Life is what you make it. You can dwell on the bad and think about all that went wrong or could go wrong. Or you can make a choice to turn your thoughts to pushing forward, utilizing the tools you are learning to keep strengthening your mindset. Your thoughts about yourself and life is your mindset. Take care of that and think the best of yourself.

Your attitude is up to you.

Having a can-do attitude helps you focus on solutions, and having a positive mental attitude affects your outlook on your day-to-day life. Having joy is always an option. Find the music, talks, quotes and poems that bring happiness and a spark in your attitude. Have some fun-- laughter is the best medicine. Choose joy.

Be a Champion of Resilience Mentality

Get up when you're knocked down.

Something, someone or some situation will inevitably come that will knock you down. Process the emotions of it, let them out and think your way through. Trust your instincts and use wisdom to see your way back up. Take a break and come to terms with it; just get back up. The only time you fail is when you stop trying. Use your tools to keep you moving forward.

What you focus on will expand.

The way to be resilient is often found in the thoughts you focus on. If you keep focusing on the problem, it will become bigger and bigger in your mind, sometimes taking on a life of its own. Shift the focus to actions going forward and the positive things you can do to turn it around. Focus on possibilities and goals, visualizing success. Let that continue to expand.

Feel what you feel, allowing emotion.

Again, the only way out is through. Face it, feel it and let the emotions come out. It is healing! Find the right place to do this and avoid getting stuck in the emotions. Feel them, let them out and realize how normal it is to feel these things. Focused thoughts will get you back to a centered and productive place that will propel you forward in a positive way.

Use logic to strengthen your mindset.

After the emotions are processed and expressed, use logic to bring you back to the present. It can be overwhelming, especially when difficult things come up in life, but if you express the emotion and use logic to move forward it will get you to that growth mindset that will produce good feelings.

See what you learned from it.

Another way to be resilient in a healthy way is to see all that you learned from the situation. Taking time to appreciate the growth can help you bounce back and even be a better person. It may not seem that way in the middle of the situation, but eventually you will start to see what you learned and the good that can come from something that was difficult.

Remember when you succeeded at overcoming.

When we draw upon past successes at overcoming the tough times, we can see that we have what it takes to make it through. We approach it with confidence and draw on the strength we have inside us. Remember what worked and visualize yourself coming through the trial.

Focus on feeding your mind positivity.

Give your mind good thoughts to work with and it will start looking for ways to overcome and bounce back from setbacks in a positive way. Push out thoughts that keep you stuck and produce negative emotions. Replace negative thoughts with what could be and what will be. You deserve a happy life and will achieve it by not giving up. Be determined, you are worth it!

You are important and have purpose.

Tap into your purpose, even if it is a slight glimmer that you see when you are experiencing a down day or in a slump. Feed your thoughts with your passions and potential. Feel how loved you are and know you are important. It will help you get back up and keep trying when you remember your infinite worth and start fueling yourself with your passion again.

Doesn't kill you makes you stronger.

The saying, "What doesn't kill you makes you stronger," may seem crass or even negative. When you come through the fire of the trial and look back, you will see that you are indeed stronger. Remind yourself and approach this trial with assurance that it is part of your growing process and it is making you stronger because you are facing it and using your tools to push forward.

50

Experiences endured prepare for future opportunities.

The growing lessons of life's experiences and what you have endured will be a blessing for someone else or even yourself to draw on in the future. You have purpose and you have everything in you to endure this trial and face what needs facing. Your mindset shifts when you see purpose for the trial and then you can better face it. Believe it will triumph and that good will come of this.

Embrace Your Differences and Unique Self

Own your quirks and understand weaknesses.

Own your quirks and unique personality. It is freeing, and you attract more into your life. People love an authentic person. Avoid measuring yourself from your weaknesses but understand what they are. It can help you be wise when making commitments. Know that those weaknesses can even become strengths one day, just be in the moment and real with where you are now.

Make a list of your strengths.

Take your time and develop a list of all your wonderful strengths. Exhaust all your efforts to see every possible strength you have seen in yourself and that others have seen in you. Remember your successes and attributes that helped you achieve each success. Listing all your strengths helps you see all you have to work with and contributes to a positive self-image.

53

Take personality test building on talents.

Personality tests are a great resource to draw out your strengths and talents. A personality test can help reveal your strengths and how to use them for your personal growth and living out your purpose. The results will outline how to build on your strengths and develop your talents to live your best life. A good comprehensive test to start with is at GallupStrengthCenter.com.

54

Look in mirror, talking to yourself.

This might be uncomfortable at first, but you are the person you will be with the rest of your life. Give yourself love and pep talks. Get comfortable encouraging yourself and believing in yourself, because that is how you will succeed. Take a minute to see you, believe in your abilities and claim your purpose so you can live it. Be your biggest ally and best friend.

55

It is healthy to love yourself.

What you feel about yourself exudes to others, whether you realize it or not. When you have a love for yourself and a healthy respect for who you are, you hold your head high and have a positive outlook and others respond to that. You show people how to treat you by the way you see yourself. It is healthy to love yourself and be at peace with who you are.

Have alone times for inner strength.

Taking time to fill yourself up with strength is important. Even five minutes alone can keep you centered and fill your inner strength. Time alone, away from the hectic things that may be going on around you, will help you stay focused and not get pulled into any chaos. Nurturing yourself is a way to sort through things, get connected with your strengths and forge ahead.

Write about ideas and your passion.

Writing about your ideas and passion will fuel more passion and build on your dreams. Thinking about what things you would like to do or try and how you could achieve them is great, and putting them on paper helps give birth to the ideas and bring them to life. It ignites more enthusiasm and builds on your ideas, even making your dreams bigger as you put things in motion and act them out.

58

Find what brings you true joy.

When have you felt true joy and happiness? Not the happiness that goes away the next day, but the happiness that fills your soul and gives you true joy. As you discover all the things that bring you that fulfilling sense of joy, be sure to take time to have more of that in your life. Life is meant to be enjoyed. Bring back the laughter and lighten things up.

# Nurture yourself with what gives energy.

Filling your soul with energy is key in building a growth mindset. Think about what brings energy into your life--prayer, reading, meditating, walking, being in nature? Who are you around, what are your surroundings and activities when you are feeling your best and getting fed emotionally? Tap into what gives you strength and energy often, it keeps you moving forward in a healthy way.

Say affirmations and act on them.

Affirmations are positive statements about yourself. They help you stay positive and claim your inner strength. For example: I am healthy, I am driven, etc. Write down your affirmations, then for each one, write an action that goes with it. Putting an action to your affirmation leads to better results. Acknowledging your growth each day adds to your positive self-image and helps build on your strengths.

Seek Help and Implement Advice Wisely

Hire a coach who strengthens you.

Coaches are valuable and can help you see things differently in a positive way. A good coach will challenge limiting beliefs and help you cultivate a growth mindset through looking at your focused thoughts that are holding you back and processing negative emotions in a way that gets you back to what you can control--your thoughts and actions. They also provide tools that push you forward toward your dreams.

Find a mentor who gets you.

Saying things out loud with a wise mentor can release a lot, and help you see situations more clearly. Gleaning on a mentor's wisdom and experiences will produce better results in your life. Speaking your thoughts and sharing things you are going through in a safe environment with people who have your best interest at heart is very helpful. It's important that you feel understood and challenged to move forward.

Be around those who give strength.

Be selective in choosing your inner circle of friends and associates. Protect yourself the best you can with a positive environment and a supportive network. Charles "Tremendous" Jones said, "You are the same today that you are going to be five years from now except for two things: the people with whom you associate and the books you read."

Ponder on advice, follow with wisdom.

Apply the things you are learning and the advice you are getting with wisdom. Using your intellect and wisdom to implement the things that make sense and challenge you is an important component to growth. Never blindly follow, seek out the wisdom, ponder and meditate on it if you need to, and accept the challenge to see things differently when you can tell it is taking you farther down the path of progress.

Be selective with whom you share.

Telling your frustration or situation to anyone who will listen is obviously not a good idea. You never know how people are going to respond to your situation and it can become another hurdle when they respond in a nonsupportive way. Seek and find the right supportive people and mentors who get you and will offer empathy, encouragement and strength.

Read books that uplift and inspire.

Feed your mind with positive books, music, and entertainment that give you strength, good energy and light. Bringing dark themes and negative influences into your mind is detrimental. You are taking an active part in your strength base and growth mindset, which requires extra effort and surrounding yourself with uplifting things that inspire growth.

Develop your tools for moving forward.

As you are being coached and or mentored by others who have strength, success and wisdom to offer, take note of the books, processes and other things that helped them and that you connect with. Develop your bank of tools that will help you move forward, then continue to use them.

Give yourself time to progress daily.

Everything takes time, and you are on a journey of personal growth, continually progressing. If you want to live with a growth mindset and as your greater self, take it one step at a time and enjoy the journey as you progress. Focus your thoughts and use the tools you are acquiring. Move forward with intention. Trust and believe that your inner strength is showing up every day and you are evolving.

Consistently use processes you have learned.

Avoid stopping processes before they become habits. Keep building on your progress and moving forward. There are ups and downs in life and you are building your strength base which will keep life's challenges from rocking your world. As you apply these processes, they will become habits that keep your mindset and inner strength intact.

Right people will appear when needed.

You will be amazed how the right people at the right time will show up to help you. You have so much inner strength and there is plenty of strength to lean on (not rely on) in your weaker moments. Most people are generous and kind. Believe it and attract that goodness to you. You will be that for someone else too as you push through life with a growth mindset.

Set and Achieve Goals on Purpose

Visualize your desired result and outcome.

Visualize yourself at the end, achieving the goal. Get that image clear in your mind. Think of all the things you will be doing and experiencing and see yourself doing it. Feel what it feels like to achieve it. If you decide it is going to happen, and put action to the thoughts, you will set about doing the very things required to bring about your desired result and make it a reality.

See what it takes to achieve.

If you know all the steps required, that's great. If not, research and study it. Talk to other people who have accomplished the same things you want to accomplish, asking what they did to achieve their goals. Read stories of people reaching the same goals and glean from their wisdom and experience.

Break goals down into three actions.

When you know what you need to work on and the actions you need to take, be wise about the starting point and break it down into the first three actions. It may take more actions than three, but beginning with three actions is less overwhelming than taking on all the tasks at once. Continue the process, building on each achievement until you have reached your goal.

Three ways to complete three actions

For each of your three actions, break them into three ways to achieve each one. For example, if your goal is a work promotion and your first action is "increase sales," break that into three ways to increase sales: (1) call leads, (2) set up appointments, and (3) follow up. With increased focus on how to achieve each action, you have a plan that can work.

75

Can't change past, only moving forward.

What you focus on expands, and there is nothing you can do about the past, so you can stop thinking about that right away. Past setbacks and failures are in the past, there is no sense revisiting them and dwelling on the negative. You learned from them, now put your focus and energy on moving forward. Hope comes when you focus on what can be and what you are working toward.

Forgive yourself for any past setbacks

Forgive yourself for past mistakes and setbacks so you can move on. Realize that you are not perfect, no one is, and failure is not final until you stop getting back up. Forgiving yourself is sometimes the hardest thing to do, but it brings renewal and more hope in your soul and provides a positive way to move forward. You are worth multiple second chances.

Believe in yourself, see yourself accomplishing.

If your mind can see it and you believe you can do it, then you will. Firm belief in yourself is more than half the battle, it is everything. Believe you can do it and you will figure out how because you will have the strength and determination. As you build on that belief which fuels your passion, you start seeing yourself accomplishing your goal, which makes it a possibility.

If you get off track, reassess.

As you are working toward your goals, you may get off track or notice it isn't working. Don't sweat it, reassess what is not working and think it through. You will see what needs changing and you will have your new starting point with that action. The key is to keep moving forward, trying out all the ways you can accomplish your goal. Persistence will get you there, never give up!

79

Celebrate the achievement when it's complete.

Take time to own your accomplishment and celebrate your achievement, even the little victories along the way to reaching the end goal. Seeing what you achieved adds to your confidence and positive self-image. It helps you move forward, face the ups and downs, and build on each achievement and the personal growth it brings. This continues to build your inner strength.

80

Reach your goals, set some more.

Now that you have accomplished your goal, keep going forward. You are becoming the person you envisioned and developing your talents. Your weaknesses are beginning to become strengths as you work on them. Keep going, keep building, reach high and know your worth. Don't stop believing and achieving!

Be Comfortable with Success. Own it!

Allow yourself a new peaceful lifestyle.

Think about the new lifestyle you are creating and embrace the peaceful feeling it brings to your soul. Allow yourself a new way of living that is not tied to the negative feelings of the past. Embrace the way it feels when things are working out and you are achieving your goals.

Avoid traps of old belief systems.

Old belief systems may creep back in and try to stop your progress. Be vigilant to not let them take hold. Use your positive affirmations and keep the vision of your desired outcome. See what you have already achieved and accomplished by applying yourself. Build on your strengths that you have discovered and the talents you are developing. Protect your thoughts, they activate behavior.

Adjust to new feeling without chaos.

Sometimes people cling to what is comfortable and if you have been in a bad place for long periods of time you might be more used to feeling unrest. Feel the peace and fulfillment from your hard work of developing a growth mindset and moving forward intentionally. You will get used to how life without chaos feels be able to bounce back more easily from down days that might come.

Expect good things coming your way.

What you put out there and how you see things creates your reality. Expect the good in the world that is coming your way and invite more of it. Stay in that positive and growth mindset that sees the possibilities of a fulfilled, peaceful, successful life.

Claim and take in the accolades

Be present, and take in the accolades and pats on the back you are getting. It is a sign of good self-confidence and maturity when you can appreciate your success. You can do this in a way that is not puffed up or self-serving, rather it is appreciating your hard work, and being O.K. with the praise. You will find the place where you are comfortable with success.

Life is what you make it.

You are making your life better by intentional living, reprogramming beliefs, forgiving, and putting your goals in action. Keep moving forward and build the life you want for yourself and your prosperity. Keep moving forward, carving out your best life one thought at a time, one decision at a time. Believe you are worth it--YOU ARE!

Continue to learn and be educated.

Keep your mind active and engaged in learning. It furthers your development, makes you and life more interesting and improves your general outlook. Whether it is a degree, certificate or continued education for your job, you'll be glad you are dedicated to learning because it advances you in more ways than one.

Show others how to treat you.

When you have a healthy self-image and carry yourself with confidence, people in general will respond with respect. If they do not respond or treat you with respect, stay centered with your inner strength and growth mindset. Pay attention to your boundaries with those in your circle of continual contact. Avoid saying negative things about yourself and don't play small to make others feel more comfortable.

89

Gain a healthy respect for yourself.

Part of owning your success is having a healthy respect for yourself. Also, each success will contribute to your self-respect and positive self-image. Respecting yourself is important for many reasons. It attracts the right partner and friends that will respect you and treat you well. Self-respect guides your attitude and brings positive things into your life.

Think big and live to achieve.

Thinking big focuses your thoughts on the big ideas and desires, and what you want to achieve in life. Stretch your dreams to be even bigger. Build your way there by putting things in motion, through your daily actions and living to achieve your dreams. Conceive it in your mind and make it a part of you, then it will begin to come to fruition.

Give Back to Community and Others

91

Priorities: always put loved ones first.

The more you grow, accomplish and achieve, you will naturally want to give back and help others do the same. Keep your immediate family, extended family and close friends as your highest priorities. Giving back to them is so fulfilling because most likely these are the very people who supported you in the tough times.

92

Living less selfishly is a blessing.

Being selfLESS is a blessing because you are enriching the lives of others and your own life is enriched as well. When your focus and intentions are for another person, something natural happens. When you help others, you yourself grow too. You will notice the warm feeling you get in your heart when you think of someone else and serve them. It is fulfilling to give, depleting to be selfish.

Donate items instead of throwing away.

Another great way to serve others and give back is to donate. You may have items that are gently used and still functioning, but if you are no longer using them, they can be a huge blessing and benefit to someone else. Repurposing goods is always more useful and generous. Thinking of others is a sign of the abundance mentality you are creating.

Many hands make the work lighter.

When more people volunteer and work together it creates synergy and projects are completed in a timelier manner. It adds to the sense of community and uplifts everyone's spirits. Your church or community may ask for help with projects in town or for a family; be quick to join in.

95

When you are hurting, reach out.

Sometimes the best way to get over a bad day or week is to find a way to help someone else out. Reaching out can get you out of your own head and release some of the heavy feelings you might be experiencing. It switches the focus to something productive and worthwhile. You clear out the darkness that might be coming back in by actively doing a good deed.

Give service to those who serve.

Take time to reach out to first responders and people you know who are actively serving others. They really appreciate it because they know the value of service and it is so uplifting to see their reaction on the receiving end. You may know a caretaker who expends all their energy helping others you could reach out to and uplift.

Improve community through outreach volunteer opportunities.

Improving where you live gives you pride in your community and fellowship with your neighbors. Look for opportunities to clean up the parks, pick up litter along the roads, remove graffiti, or any other needs in your community. You will be recognized as a leader when you pitch in and you will make associations with like-minded people.

98

See a need, try to accommodate.

Giving back and serving others gives your life depth and meaning. When you see a need, try to accommodate it. Whether it is giving up a seat on a crowded bus for a pregnant woman or elderly person, or paying the difference at a checkout line for the person who is short and can't cover their bill. Pay it forward and see how good it feels.

Respond with compassion first and uplift.

When noticing the needs of others around you, you may find someone who needs your help, but they may behave abruptly or show a lot of negative emotion. Respond with compassion first and realize you are not going to be around this person very long. Do what you can to uplift them while you are in their presence. They are in pain and your compassion will have an impact on them.

100

Share your wisdom and give encouragement.

The wisdom you have gained from working on these *Forward Principles* will help you be even stronger when facing new trials that may come your way. Even more, you are equipped with life's lessons and experiences to share on personal development. You can truly encourage other people. As James M. Barrie said, "Those who bring sunshine into the lives of others cannot keep it from themselves."

Six-Word Lessons for a Growth Mindset

Note from the Author

I would love to hear from you, so please share your story with me. It would be an honor to work with you, encouraging and supporting you with *Forward Principles*.

On my website, **ForwardPrinciples.com**, you will find the following tools to help you in your journey:

> **Mindset Motivator** offers motivational messages of enlightenment, and gives you access to **Weekly Warrior** sessions to keep *Forward Principles* at the top of your mind, and a **Monthly Power Hour** to dive deeper into principles, tools and techniques to keep you moving forward in a positive way.

I have given motivational speeches to women's groups, corporations, political, domestic violence and abuse support groups, and at retreats.

I am also the author of *Six-Word Lessons to Overcome Abuse and Adversity*.

Contact me at RaeAnn@ForwardPrinciples.com
425-218-8277
PO Box 662, Mukilteo, WA 98275

About the Six-Word Lessons Series

Legend has it that Ernest Hemingway was challenged to write a story using only six words. He responded with the story, "For sale: baby shoes, never worn." The story tickles the imagination. Why were the shoes never worn? The answers are left up to the reader's imagination.

This style of writing has a number of aliases: postcard fiction, flash fiction, and micro fiction. Lonnie Pacelli was introduced to this concept in 2009 by a friend, and started thinking about how this extreme brevity could apply to today's communication culture of text messages, tweets and Facebook posts. He wrote the first book, *Six-Word Lessons for Project Managers*, then he and his wife Patty started helping other authors write and publish their own books in the series.

The books all have six-word chapters with six-word lesson titles, each followed by a one-page description. They can be written by entrepreneurs who want to promote their businesses, or anyone with a message to share.

See the entire *Six-Word Lessons Series* at **6wordlessons.com**

www.ingramcontent.com/pod-product-compliance
Lightning Source LLC
Chambersburg PA
CBHW062008070426
42451CB00008BA/277